Rings and Things

Thoughts of a *Man's* ~~House~~wife

by

<small>GRACE RUSSELL</small>

illustrated by

<small>GORDON HAUG</small>

UR—243—10-0470
Printed in the United States of America

To HANK
and our CHILDREN
I dedicate this book

With a note of deep appreciation
to VIRGINIA WALTERS
who typed my manuscript
to our TUESDAY PRAYER GROUP
who encouraged me to proceed
and most of all
to GOD
who made me want to write it
and to my PARENTS
who introduced me to Him
when I was still a child

CONTENTS

Preface

I must confess that the vocation of housewife—by that I mean its nitty-gritty, daily drudgery—is really not my cup of tea.

I admit it with some chagrin since it seems less than feminine; and I have this feeling that other women might really get a kick out of scrubbing floors, polishing silver, ironing mountains of clothes, and repeating the million-and-one other details necessary to keep a household running smoothly.

There are, however, other aspects of the calling that I do enjoy, like sleeping with a handsome husband who after more years than I care to mention still makes me feel like a bride, having babies and watching them grow through all the interesting stages of human development—sharing their laughter and tears, their fears and aspirations, their work and fun.

I love the coziness of a warm fire on a cold night, the gaiety of birthdays and Christmas, and the company of friends. In fact, I love all that warm aura that makes a house a home. I am, admittedly, far more Mary than Martha; but Martha's chores must be done; and I know a way to make them not only endurable, but rewarding as well.

The truth is that your hands can do those things about which Martha must be anxious and still leave your Mary-like heart free to kneel at the feet of the Master.

Hope in My Heart

Of all the thoughts my mind does think

When standing by my kitchen sink,

The ones which most enrich my soul

And touch my heart to make it whole

Are those which come in deepest prayer

To make me sure that God is there,

And that whatever life may bring

He'll take my heart and make it sing!

1. *Marriage-Keeping*

I rather resent being labeled "housewife." I married no house. I married a man and am far more interested in *marriage-keeping* than *housekeeping*. So are all my friends; yet I have seen many a marriage go down the drain as accidentally as my sterling butterknife which slipped unnoticed into the drain of my sink, or be as mutilated as those teaspoons which have inadvertently found their way into the disposal. In both cases I was more concerned with getting the dishes done than preserving the silver. Sometimes in keeping a house we wives forget the husbands and children we keep those houses for.

Few marriages are made on the basis of housekeeping aptitude. They are made because two people find themselves caught up in that magic attraction of young love

which makes every day a day of glory. Each finds in the other that which makes life complete. It is the maintenance of the spiritual glow of love in the heart that is the essential ingredient of a happy home.

Being so easily entangled in the mundane routines of life makes keeping romance alive more than is humanly possible without the reinforcement of the love of God in the heart. After all, love is God's invention, not our own. It must be polished with forgiveness, hope, and laughter, and handled with the care it so deserves.

Read Proverbs 31:10-31.

Dear Lord,

As I busily go about the tasks required to keep our house, let me always remember that love alone is the foundation of a happy and enduring home. Keep my heart open to Your joy and gladness so I will be fun to live with and worthy of my husband's love. For Jesus' sake. Amen.

2. *Ajax and Incense*

I firmly believe that God speaks to every individual according to his capacity to hear. He is not limited to the hallowed sanctuary nor the mountain height.

I know this to be true because He has spoken to me. How He does this is for God to know and me to wonder, but He has guided my thoughts in many ways in many places.

I have heard His voice in the melody of a birdcall, in the greenness of a blade of grass reaching toward the sun, in the stillness of the evening, in the warm embrace of love, and the twinkle in the eye of a mischievous child.

If God so permeates all things, who are we to consider one task holy and another menial?

The knee is just as bent in scrubbing bathrooms as in kneeling for communion, and with practice the heart can be just as attuned to God's voice in one place as in another. I admit it is easier in some places. I love the exhilarating hush of a holy worship hour, the light through stained glass windows, the minister's voice, and the perfumed presence of other worshipers in God's house. In this holy place it is easy to commune with God and have my soul cleansed.

At home scrubbing bathrooms with the chlorine smell of Ajax stinging my nose, it is more difficult, but not impossible, to so commune.

If in this, my most obnoxious chore, God is able to speak to me, then life is good, for no matter how I may hate the mechanics of a task it cannot separate me from the love of God; and often He uses these very chores like words as vehicles of truth.

Read John 13:3-15.

Dear Lord,

I thank You for being accessible to me wherever I am. Your presence with me even in those chores of life which I find distasteful and uninteresting helps me to realize that You are near in all life's circumstances, and this gives me hope and confidence for myself and all Your other children. I remember how You washed the disciples' feet and thus set us an example of service. Help me never to lose sight of the significance of service in Your great scheme of things. Amen.

3. *Words to Work By*

Perhaps the greatest single side benefit of housework from a spiritual point of view is its boredom.

This may sound ridiculous, but the repetitious boredom of household routines lends them to muscular habits which require little thought and thus free the mind to wander— provided, of course, that the TV and radio are turned down low enough and the noise of machinery is not too distracting.

This mental freedom is matched by few occupations outside a convent; and the Christian housewife can—if she chooses—spend many hours a day in meditation and prayer, nourishing her soul with God's love in order to equip herself to spread His love to others.

Read Philippians 4:8.

Dear Lord,

As my hands are busy about the many things with which they must be busy if I make a good home for those I love, let my mind be busy with the things that make a home for You in all our hearts. In Your name I pray. Amen.

4. *Coffee*

As usual I cleaned the percolator, measured the water and the coffee grounds, and went about my routine of buttering bread and frying bacon, cooking oatmeal and setting the table.

At first I did not notice the silence, and then I realized that the bubbling perk of the coffeepot was not playing its accompaniment to the sizzling skillet. Looking around, I realized that the cord was not plugged in.

I was struck with the metaphor, for all too often other lives and my own are carefully groomed and educated but fail to perk because the power of God is not at work there. Too often we are just not plugged in to the power of God.

Read Ephesians 3.

Dear Lord,

As I go about my work today, help me to stay plugged in to Your power. Let me not just occupy a space on life's shelf, but let me this day accomplish the purpose for which I was designed. May the lovely rhythm of Your music perk up my life and sing through me this day. Amen.

5. *Jane of All Trades*

In this overspecialized and automated world, the term "Jack of all trades" is fast becoming obsolete. Only a few vocations even *allow,* much less *require,* a versatility of talents. One of these few is the vocation of *housewife.* The demand for versatility in this calling makes "Jane of all trades" more accurate.

A housewife must be teacher, glamour girl, physician, nurse, scrubwoman, chef, seamstress, painter, interior decorator, purchasing agent, economist, beautician, electrician, gardener, designer, conversationalist, public relations officer, laundress, playmate, and a companion among other things. Anyone with one eye and half sense can tell at a glance that no woman is paragon of virtue enough to be adequate in all these areas. So perhaps more than anyone else the housewife really needs the eternal adequacy of God to make her capable of coping with her role in life.

Upon visiting an American kitchen, a Korean college student told me, "I didn't realize that American housewives had to be electrical engineers as well, but you'd have to be to operate all this machinery."

American housewives have also wondered if the time saved by all these gadgets is really any better spent running car pools, chairing endless committees, or watching TV's trivia in exhaustion.

Amidst the buzzing of the motors, the ring of the phone, the call of all who make a claim on her time, it is sometimes hard for the harried housewife to hear the still small voice of God. Yet Christ still speaks those eternally comforting words, "Come unto me . . . and I will give you rest."

Read Matthew 11:28-30.

Dear Lord,

I am so weary with all the details of running a household that my back aches, my head reels, and I feel utterly exhausted. Surely much of this running about is unnecessary. I come to You, Lord, with my busy, unimportant day and pray that You will let me exchange it for Your light and easy yoke that will give me rest in my soul.

It is my competitive spirit that makes me hurry so, Lord. I want my house to be cleaner, my children to be smarter, my committees to run smoother to prove my capability to myself and others. How foolish can I get, Lord? These little things that so encumber me are very trivial. I lay them at Your feet and pray that You will make me quit trying to excel and become instead a source of Your love and quiet joy to those I am privileged to serve, that I may gradually become a little bit like You. Amen.

14

6. *Freedom*

There is no freedom. He who seeks it is a fool. Man's only choice is that of what he will serve. In the political realm he may choose what he calls freedom, but he thereupon must of necessity accept the burden of individual responsibility. He may seek freedom from his conscience; but he therefore loses his power of choice and deposits the responsibility for his acts within the church with its imposed penances and reprisals, or with the state with its rigid laws and punishment for the breach of them.

Freedom is both an illusion and a farce. It is shouted by demagogue and mouthed by clergy and sought after by the common man. Freedom from moral restraints has as its counterpart bondage to sin. Freedom from worry has as its counterpart bondage to passiveness. Freedom from responsibility in any realm carries with it by its very nature a bondage to those who shoulder responsibility.

The only semblance of freedom lies in man's freedom to choose the truth as he sees it, the good as he understands it—to accept of his own free will the responsibilities that go with any way of life, shouldering those encumbrances, laughing at the load, and enjoying whatever measure of happiness that can be gleaned from each day's experience.

The only freedom man has any control over is freedom from the conflict within himself. He can only achieve this when he looks the conflict squarely in the eye, seeks not a perfect solution, but the best one open to him under the circumstances, and abides by his decision, never looking back.

Read Joshua 24:15; Luke 16:13; 9:23.

Dear Lord,

Help us to exercise our freedom of spirit wisely in choosing that which we will serve. Give us the freedom that comes only with turning all that we are and have completely over to You. For Jesus' sake. Amen.

7. *This One Thing I Do*

On my more efficient days—I use the comparative rather than the superlative because my days are almost never superlatively efficient—I plan to accomplish one major purpose and let the details assume minimal importance. This is a freeing device that works well for me.

Any woman knows that her days can never be wholly devoted to one task because families must be fed, telephones must be answered, and routine chores must be at least haphazardly accomplished; but to have one emphasis rather than half a dozen is a big help. Not only this, but having one goal for the day offers a much better chance of successful completion of that *one* thing, and thus a chance to savor that delicious sense of accomplishment that can only come with a difficult task well done.

To some extent the span of our life, too, is better oriented if we have one major purpose. I heard a record once made by a young man who set as his goal becoming a millionaire and retiring before he was thirty-five. He had just retired at that age a multimillionaire. He felt confident that the explanation of his success lay in the fact that he set this one goal early in life and worked consistently toward it from then on.

Perhaps the reason I remember the gist of his record so well is because at the time I heard it I was toying with a number of equally tantalizing possible goals to pursue.

I was already well into my life as a minister's wife, but I longed to do something really *worthwhile*. At that moment I was seriously considering writing a book, taking a job as art supervisor for the local school system, or returning to college to work on a graduate degree.

The truth of the matter was that as the empty-nest phase of motherhood loomed before me I realized I was going to feel empty and unneeded in the very near future. For several days I could not get that this-one-thing-I-do theme out of my mind, and in periods of prayer I sat down and asked God to help me determine which *one thing* was His will for me.

Strangely enough, He showed me which *one thing* He required of me; and it was none of the above. As I read and thought and prayed, I became impressed with the fact that the one thing around which I must orient my life was being a channel for the love of God to flow through to other people, whoever and wherever they may be.

It was like having my eyes suddenly opened. I became aware every day of the people who were desperately seeking a workable faith. In realizing that the vessel is not important, but what it contains, I became free and open and found it easy to communicate the love of God to other people regardless of their age, temperament, or background; and it all came about not through my seeking them out, but being available when they came to me.

This happened a few months ago; and here I find myself finally writing that book, which is one way to communicate this love of God. I am teaching art to a class of doctors' wives on a relaxed schedule that does not interfere with my other duties as a wife and mother—and I have felt the love of God flow among the members of this class. I am sure that one of these days we will live near enough to a graduate school for me to pursue that extra degree if God deems it necessary for me to have one.

In orienting the short day of my life again around this central purpose which seems to be God's call for me, I find that life is far more varied and satisfying without all that distraught feeling of having gotten up early each morning to ride my horse off in all directions. The mundane duties that are so daily become minor details, and the light of living shines in the shared moments of inspiration that unfailingly come as God allows my life to cross the lives of others.

Read Philippians 3:13-14.

Dear Lord,

I thank You for the sense of wholeness in my soul that has come since You showed me that all the varied activities of my life have purpose when viewed as opportunities through which Your love may flow through me into the lives of others. All the loose ends seem to fall into place since life's central purpose for me has been revealed. Use me as You choose, Lord, for I would rather be doing a *little* thing made glorious by Your presence than a self-important *nothing* of my own. Amen.

8. *Lists*

Not often are the dishwasher, washer, dryer, mixer, TV, and radio silent at the same time in our house. The quiet ticking of the clock is seldom the only noise that breaks the silence; and because we are so accustomed to its rhythmic ticking, we hardly notice as it marks off the minutes and the hours. Only when it strikes to call attention to itself do I remember it is there.

Time passes on. The fleeting moments in which we will to do and do not glide by soundlessly, leaving a void.

Laughter comes with achievement. Love comes with thoughtful deeds of concern for others. These things take time. To do what you want to for yourself is not always the best, nor at last even the easiest way to use time. To dwell with God—to know life at its fullest—is to have duties to perform, work to do, challenges to meet. Youth passes, but God is still the same, and life in His keeping can still be good.

Time is the one thing that comes to each of us daily in equal measure. I have the same amount of time each Monday that is granted to presidents or queens. Obviously it is not the amount of time we have but how we manage it that matters.

The only way I have ever found to manage time is to plan my days. Even if I have to forsake the plan completely as more pressing duties call, I get more done that I need to do than if I wander aimlessly from one thing to another.

My first week at college a teacher gave me in one sentence a pointer that has proved more practical for life than most of that semester's courses. She told the girls in her dorm, "Learn to make a schedule and follow it."

For years now I have made my daily list and have for the most part managed to get most of the things on it done, even if I carried chores over to the next day's list time after time.

It has been said by wiser ones than I that we do what we want to do. If you doubt this, try making out a schedule for a week and see how many of the things you dread are simply left off your list.

Read Psalm 90:12.

19

Dear Lord,

As we make our daily lists of life, let us not leave off the things You would have us do. Help us not to cram each minute so full of trivialities that we leave no time to feel the warmth of Your sunshine, to see the beauty of the world around us, or to lend a helping hand to one in need. For Jesus' sake. Amen.

9. People

There is nothing more interesting than people. I think sometimes the friends we know are like a vast library. Some of them are so intent upon their privacy that their pages are stuck together and you can never read what is inside. Others carry the dominant factors of their stories on their covers, in the expressions on their faces.

The library written in the hearts of people is full of tales of tragedy, heroism, patriotism, faith. There are comedies and satires, discoveries, conquests, research. Every life has a pattern and a plot; and the reading is so varied and inexhaustible, so full of information and inspiration that no one need ever be bored or without purpose or hope.

Jesus said, "The kingdom of God is within you"; and it is truly within this library of people who cross our paths every day. The only trouble is that to read here we must use our ears as well as our eyes. The pages must be turned with sympathy, and the passages must be underlined with the heart.

As is the case with any library, the more one reads the more he understands. The inklings of the truth that come from one book added to those that come from another enlarge the base of truth upon which we build the structures of our lives. We miss more than we can possibly imagine if we fail to recognize the spirit of God at work in the lives of other people.

Read Colossians 3:16.

Dear Lord,

I thank You for letting me see in the lives of other people the beauty and majesty of Your presence. I thank You for the depth of faith in the lives of those with whom I have taken time to talk. There is nothing quite so strengthening as the sharing of the faith. Let me not walk through the library of life and fail to read the books I pass. For Jesus' sake. Amen.

10. *Loneliness*

There is a loneliness that fills the human heart no matter how surrounded one may be with people if he feels estranged from God. Most of us pass through such periods from time to time in our lives and come to feel that a God, no matter how tyrannical, is to be preferred above a void in space.

In seeking to make God what he wants Him to be, man forgets that it is he who is molded by God and not vice versa.

A God whose will depends entirely upon man's willingness to cooperate is no God at all. Those who so limit God will never really understand His power.

We are lonely if we seek only a powerless, man-conceived idea of God. We need God Himself, the maker and preserver of the universe, the giver of immortal life.

This I Believe

God is.

God cares.

God does not expect human perfection—He knows us too well for that.

It is only in going beyond legalities and into love that man can ever find himself.

It is only in going beyond the call of duty that we can find joy.

God's disciplines may for a time seem difficult to bear, but in the long run His ways are sure.

Man is never more imperfect than when he seeks his own perfection.

He is never more selfish than when unselfishness is his goal.

He is never more unloving than when he fails to love himself.

Man is made in the image of God.

To deny that image is to destroy himself.

God never demands the impossible, for all things are possible with His help. Paul wrote, "I can do all things through Christ which strengtheneth me."

Here are a few rules we ought to live by:

Love yourself—otherwise you cannot love your neighbor.

Live for a purpose greater than yourself—live so you can truly say, "For me to live is Christ."

Forget yourself: "He that loseth his life for my sake shall find it."

Having found a faith that will support us in life's extremities, let us not desert it when tempted to think we can manage life alone, for:

> God's ways are higher than our ways;
> He can see down the road ahead.
> Though the way may be uphill and tiring,
> Someday we will know where it led.
> There are valleys on every horizon;
> Without them no mountains could be.
> All our world would be shut in and stifling,
> With no high points from which we could see.
> Love others with cheerful abandon,
> But keep God on the throne of your life.
> To try to replace Him with others
> Is only to give in to strife;
> For God will alone reassure us,
> He only can show us the way.
> We need to seek God every morning
> To walk with Him all through the day.

Read Psalm 27:1.

Dear Lord,

For Your healing presence and guiding purpose in our lives, we give You thanks. Amen.

11. *Doorbells*

Amidst the dehumanizing array of gadgets which supposedly make life easier there are few which really contribute to the strengthening of the inner resources of life. One of these few is the telephone. Another is the doorbell.

My husband thinks I always run too fast to answer either of these. Perhaps it is my woman's curiosity that makes the ring of a bell such an intriguing sound. Even in the middle of an engrossing task, I seldom find the phone's ring the bother that some people claim it is to them.

Interruptions are occasionally annoying, but a welcome voice at the other end of the line or a smiling face in my

doorway gives me such a lift that I do not mind working faster to make up for lost time after goodbyes are said.

I suppose somewhere in my heart I still remember the bustle of the big old house on Main Street where I grew up. We said it was like Grand Central Station, and it was.

It repeated itself in a succession of small-town homes with neighbors always dropping in. Now that we are on the very edge of suburbia that phone is my heart line to people, and to tell the truth I love it. The doorbell, too, signals me to meet a friend.

Read John 15:12-17.

Dear Lord,

I am bad about taking the technological triumphs of the twentieth century for granted. Thank You for making a world where these things are possible. Bless those who have the urge to invent things. Inspire them and reveal to them the truths upon which all inventions rest. Bless those of us who benefit by them that we may use them wisely and well—to build bridges of love toward our fellowman. For Jesus' sake. Amen.

12. *Recognition*

Long ago a wise man said, "A good name is rather to be chosen than great riches." This is true.

A good name implies that one *has* a name and is not just one of a nameless mass of faces in a crowd—that one *is* somebody, has certain abilities, and may be respected for what he is and what he does.

A good name, i.e., reputation, does much to enable a person to achieve. We do well as Christians to build up the good names of others and thus enrich their lives.

Our bishop makes a point of learning people's names and recognizing them by name whenever possible. This is his way of saying to his people, "You *are* somebody; you *matter* to God and to me."

In today's impersonal world we as Christians need to *know* people, to *recognize* them for what they are and thus help them see themselves as children of God, members of the most elite family there is—the only family whose ties endure forever.

Read Galatians 4:1-7.

Dear Lord,

Help us to be aware of our place as heirs of God, members of the immortal family of Christ. Help us to recognize our brothers and sisters in the faith and build them up in all good things. For Jesus' sake. Amen.

13. *The Surgery of the Spirit*

Some of us are sick some of the time, some are sick most of the time, and a few seem to be sick all the time.

Some are made so by pain or diseased tissues, and actual surgery must be performed. More often the skillful surgery of the spirit that only the great Physician can perform is what we need.

The healing of Christ has in many cases made life whole and well at its core in spite of physical disability.

This is the most difficult healing of all and can only come through a personal appointment with the great Physician. Fortunately, He keeps office hours twenty-four hours a day, wherever we are.

Read II Corinthians 4:16; Luke 4:38-40.

Dear Lord,

When life makes us sick, help us to read and heed Your prescriptions for life that will make us whole. In the great Physician's name. Amen.

14. *Frustration**

There is something in the soul of man that cries out against inertia. Man was not made to vegetate, to sit and wait—but to be active and free, to achieve. Whenever he loses his avenues of creativity and fails to achieve, his soul sickens unto death no matter how resilient his body may be. Man is more than matter. He shares something of the creative heart of God; and if this inner soul is stifled, he is miserable indeed.

I speak from sad experience, for I have known the exultation of busy creative activity and I have known the gloom and despair of inactivity. I have known the joy of anticipating gladness and the gloom of anticipating pain.

Perhaps to be sensitive to the needs of others and to be unable to succor those needs is a curse. As a curse it affects me, anyway. To long to love that which seems to be unlovely and to be unable to do so is frustration at its highest. To long to think clearly and to be unable to is disastrous to the mind.

To will to adjust and to be unable to do so is a conflict-building malady of the soul. I have found it impossible to eliminate the conflict by apathy.

My fighting spirit rebels at ease and inactivity. My soul longs to embrace each new day, live it, love it to the fullest,

---

* This was first written in pencil on paper towels during a confinement in the hospital after a wreck.

come what may. What is the secret to this way of living? What is wrong with me that I cannot find it?

Within my heart a small voice whispers: "You. You have built a fence around you—I, My, Me—until you can't climb over or crawl under or through it. Too long you have dwelt on your problems, too long confined yourself to seeking solutions where no solutions lie. Get up, go out, serve others: first of all your family, then the families of those around you. Share their sorrows and joys. Forget your own problems and soon you'll find they have vanished. God will flow through you out into life, and in His blessing others He'll bless you."

Straighten up; work hard; give generously; fear not. We are all God's and are mostly mortal. Were it not for His gift of immortality life would be drab and meaningless, but He has given us His Son to guide us in the way of eternal life. Jesus says, "Rise up and follow me."

If we, like Thomas, say, "We know not whither thou goest," He says, "Go home, do there your task and you will know that I go before you. You'll know where I go and the way you'll know."

Read Psalm 27; Matthew 10:39; 9:1-7

Dear Lord,

I thank You for speaking to me through the grogginess of my sedation and pain Your words of assurance. I tried it, Lord, and You know it has worked. I have suffered and survived the pain of the surgery I feared; and almost in spite of myself You have blessed me with many days of joy, with hosts of new friends and a depth of peace within my soul which passes understanding. Thank You, Lord. Amen.

15. *Tranquilizers Versus Tranquility*

I was cleaning out the medicine chest the other day and came across several bottles of unused tranquilizers that different doctors had prescribed during a period of real spiritual upheaval in my life. The tranquilizers had made me so unable to think through my problems that I had finally cast them aside.

Holding them in my hand, I remembered the things that had been bothering me at the time. Those little pills had not changed the circumstances one bit; and because they did not basically alter my feeling toward those problems, they offered me no relief. In fact, they deepened my sense of depression. But, thank God, I found something that did help.

I began to pray for those I felt had wronged me, at first only with my lips, but eventually with my heart; and the burdens that left me feeling incapacitated were lifted by our wonderful forgiving Lord. In the process of my misery He gave me a deeper understanding of people who also suffer in their hearts and a sensitivity to their needs that I had never had before.

I knew how it felt to fail, to lose my sense of self-esteem; but I discovered the wonderful adequacy of God's love that can use us in spite of our human frailties.

The early Communists derisively defined Christianity as the opiate of the people. They meant it as an insult, a criticism, a slap in the face; but in this day of tranquilizers, pain killers, and sleeping pills, perhaps we need to take a different look at the statement and see if hidden in the insult might have been the compliment of a recognition of an inescapable evidence of tranquility furnished by the Christian faith.

In our demanding that we not be complacent in the face of evil and injustice in the world, we Christians fail to realize how sorely the world needs to learn again what I Timothy 6:6 says, "Godliness with contentment is great gain."

Tranquility of spirit and passiveness are not synonymous. Some of the greatest leaders our world has known had at the center of their being a confidence in the goodness of God that gave them a basic tranquility. We, too, can have this central core of calm if we keep God on the throne of our lives. Instead of making us selfishly complacent, it will give us the confidence to change what we can change and the assurance that the outcome is in hands greater than our own.

Dear Lord,

I thank You that when I prayed to You in desperation You heard me and showed me that even trouble is an instrument in Your hand to mold us into more understanding people. I thank You for Your forgiveness to me, but I thank You also for showing me the joyful easing of the burdens of the heart when I was able to forgive others. Lord, it is a great relief not to feel that I have to be as perfect as possible to merit Your love. The power of Your redemption in my hour of spiritual weakness has shown me what a gracious Savior You are. I love You, Lord. Amen.

16. *The Loom*

There are many situations in life which are not easy
—the sudden changes brought about by death; the pain of
accidents, sickness, disappointment; or just the necessity
for deciding which course to take when several avenues are
open may throw us into a quandary. Many situations are
difficult to cope with, and no one can tell just what will
work, but time has taught me that God *does* take care of
things in His own good time.

I am so impatient that I want everything done immediately, but that is seldom God's way. The intricate design
of interwoven lives and experiences that He weaves into
our souls never ceases to amaze me.

So often I feel that I am pushing my own little shuttle.
It is a great relief to know that God is at the loom of our
lives, and that He can even incorporate the knots we tangle
into the threads of our days to enhance His overall pattern
for us.

Read Proverbs 3:6.

Dear Lord,

Keep me ever conscious of Your hand on the shuttle of
my life. Let me not become entangled with that which
would separate me from You, but keep me ever willing to
do Your will, to discern Your pattern for my life and to walk
in the way I should go. For Jesus' sake. Amen.

17. *Dust*

There are, of course, different degrees of clean and
dirty. A tiny layer of dust may be almost imperceptible,
but a chunk of mud is easily seen. If the light of the

sun is bright enough, the eager housewife will whisk the dust away.

Even the slattern will brush the mud aside. Only the blind to dirt will leave both where they are. When it comes to sin, many of us, unfortunately, are blind.

So what is sin? That which separates us from God. Must it always be evil? It becomes so if it takes first place in our lives. That is why selfishness and pride are so often looked upon as sins; yet, truly, self-preservation and self-esteem rightly employed are not only virtues but are essential if human life is to survive.

What then of good and evil? Some things are intrinsically good and others evil. Most things are only evil if abused. The yardsticks of ethical behavior are hidden under layers of half-truths today, but they are still around and are worth looking for.

In our eagerness to minimize the evilness of evil, we have accidentally obliterated the goodness of good.

In assuming no absolutes the measuring sticks for ethical morality have disappeared. There *are* absolute good and evil in the world, though in the lives of men they are never altogether pure. The best of human hearts are sprinkled with a little evil, and the worst of them are sprinkled with a tiny spark of good. This does not, however, eliminate the necessity of the theoretical absolutes nor make this concept irrelevant. It is the vision of God's absolute goodness that encourages us to seek the removal of the evil from our lives.

> The dust of our days falls on our souls
> And clutters them with grime.
> If we could wipe the dust away,
> We'd find a shine on them.
> The bitterness and hurts that come

With all the passing years
God's love can surely take away
With our repentant tears.
His love can take the dirt away
And polish to a gloss
And resurrect in each of us
Life's gain beyond its loss.

Read Matthew 5:48.

Dear Lord,

You know how very imperfect I am. I keep my soul as haphazardly as I keep my house and do not know how dusty it is until the keen ray of Your love pierces the darkness of my heart and shows me where the trouble is. You know far better than I that I will never come near to achieving perfection, but I thank You for reminding me that perfection should be my goal. In our perfect Redeemer's name. Amen.

18. *Patience*

For many years I prayed for patience and understanding and for a wisdom beyond my own. I never dreamed how much such blessings cost or how difficult these gifts are to unwrap.

To unwrap understanding you have to break the shiny seals of self-sufficiency and stand broken and inadequate through no apparent fault of your own. Then you do not *sympathize* with those who suffer; you *understand* their pain. You recognize the suffering in the eyes of others and can stretch out a helping hand.

Patience can never be won without waiting, yet it is a prerequisite of a sure and confident faith. Many spiritual values can only be developed by time. God uses the waiting to mold us into what He wants us to be.

Without patience and understanding there can be no true wisdom. There may be an accumulation of knowledge, but facts alone make no man truly wise.

There is an old saying, "Be careful what you pray for, you might get it." This applies to patience, understanding, and wisdom. The only way to receive them is a toilsome, thorny way; but they are well worth the struggle.

Not only do they tend to make man's soul content, but they open new doors at every turn and build bridges across the most unfathomable distances separating man from man.

Read Isaiah 40:28-31.

Dear Lord,

I still pray for greater patience, understanding, and wisdom because having come this far along life's way I am *sure* they are values that really matter. In the name of our all-wise Lord. Amen.

19. *Recipes*

There are two things I have learned about recipes. You cannot make bread without yeast or a yeast substitute to leaven the loaf, and nothing tastes good without a little salt.

Jesus picked a very heartening thing to compare us Christians to. He did not say, "You must increase in numbers in the church until you become the flour in the loaf of life." On the contrary, He said, "You are the salt,"

34

that tiny, zesty, flavorful pinch of people who change the taste of life. You are the yeast to make life's loaf light and palatable.

I am glad He spoke about the kitchen. The saltcellar thus becomes a call to prayer, and such a simple thing as bread serves as a reminder of the essence of life.

Read Matthew 5:13; Luke 13:20-21.

Dear Lord,

Help me to be a dynamic, flavorful Christian so that life will be interesting and tasty for those whose days meet mine. For Jesus' sake. Amen.

20. *Packaging*

"What's on the outside takes as much time to produce and costs almost as much as what's on the inside," I have heard friends say of packaging.

I am inclined to think they are right. Every morning I empty the tall wastebasket in my kitchen of all the empty cartons, boxes, and cans that have accumulated the preceding day. It really seems a waste to throw them away, but they are of no value if there is nothing inside.

I think we often apply the same system of things to people. As mothers we spend so much time sewing, mending, washing, ironing, shampooing, bathing, polishing shoes, and feeding bodies that we have little time left to fill our human packages with qualities of mind and personality which will make them anything more than empty cartons on the shelf of life.

35

Men must have something inside them to be of value, and the world's mothers are the ones who need to put it there. It takes God's wisdom to know what to put and in what quantities.

Read Proverbs 22:6.

Dear Lord,

Help me not to fill life's shelves with empty people; but if it becomes a matter of either/or, let me concentrate not on the package, but on what is inside both in myself and my family. For Jesus' sake. Amen.

21. *Diets*

Nobody wants to be fat. Everywhere I go everyone is concerned with the growing problem of obesity.

We want good food, well seasoned, low in cholesterol for the sake of our hearts, low in calories to keep our waistlines down—but high in those food elements that build strong and energetic bodies, that keep our cheeks rosy and guarantee to prolong our youth.

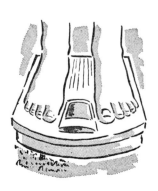

Yet the problem of obesity rises alarmingly; and in spite of our emphasis on losing weight, most of us seem to be gaining it instead. Why? The primary reason is because we pamper ourselves too much. We indulge ourselves with desserts and fried chicken and other foods and with more harmful things and wonder why our diet shows.

Our spiritual diet also shows. Jesus had a lot to say about food. He said, "Man shall not live by bread alone, but by every word that proceedeth out of the mouth of God." "Blessed are they which do hunger and thirst after righteousness: for they shall be filled."

Are we trying to satisfy our spiritual hunger by overeating the bread of the flesh?

What are the foods of the spirit? It is fitting to the mind of today's dieter to find that in the Bible the foods of the spirit are listed as fruits—fruits low in fat, low in calories, meant not to distort the personality, but full of vitamins and minerals and those things that keep the soul in trim.

Here they are: "The fruit of the Spirit is love, joy, peace, long-suffering, gentleness, goodness, faith, meekness, temperance: against such there is no law."

Jesus also practiced the self-discipline of fasting (dieting, if you please). He did not do it for His appearance's sake, but to keep His soul in shape.

Read Matthew 6:16-18.

Dear Lord,

I have trouble with my self-discipline in giving up earthly food. You know how much more difficult it is to deny myself the indulgences that make my soul get out of shape. I have trouble with my tongue, Lord, and do not always weigh my words in the scale of kindness before I speak. I pass on news that would be better stopped with me. I want my own way whether my way is best or not. I cling to bitterness and hurt feelings when they need to be thrown away. Lord, let me not nibble at the spiritual scraps of life and fatten my soul with that which does not satisfy. Keep me in trim, I pray. For Jesus' sake. Amen.

22. *Clogged Drains*

If there is anything I hate it is a clogged drain! Nothing is more exasperating than dirty dishwater that will not drain out.

We had clogged drains the other day, and it was an unpleasant and expensive experience. After much digging and cleaning, the plumber crawled out from under the house and explained that it was not a sudden thing that had happened to that drain. Little by little, over a period of months, grease had gradually adhered to the drainpipe until finally no water could go through.

He advised me to put in Drano to remove the grease or to run hot water through the pipes every few days. "Or better still," he grinned, "don't pour grease down the drain in the first place."

How like clogged drains our lives sometimes become!

We allow those things which choke out our ability to forgive to remain within us until finally we are unable to rid ourselves of all the resentments and unpleasantness and grief that accumulate to spoil our lives.

Our souls need the purging power of prayer and the warm water of love to unclog the drains and take away the evil that so easily overtakes us.

Read Ephesians 4:26.

Dear Lord,

Purge my heart of every wicked thing that would make my life a cesspool of bitterness and hate. Let Your forgiveness flush all the dross away. For Jesus' sake. Amen.

23. *Glasses*

I have spent a lot of my life making excuses for people, trying to see beneath the obvious faults some spark of spiritual greatness to be mined and tooled and shined to ornament society. Most of this delving has been worth it; and beneath many a scrubby, gravelly surface real goodness has been discovered.

Perhaps this sort of seeing is what Jesus had in mind when He said, "Having eyes, see ye not? and having ears hear ye not?" I hope He meant for us to look beyond the evil into the good and that I am not just cowardly refusing to recognize the evil that I see.

Read Romans 12:9-21.

Dear Lord,

May I look at others with the lens of love that will enable me to focus on their goodness and not the evil in their lives. Amen.

24. *Thoughts Under the Hair Dryer*

I looked at the beautifully swirled white hair the operator was arranging for the lady across from my hair dryer and at the lady's unfamiliar face in the mirror. It was lined with little wrinkles that come from too much smiling; the brow was furrowed as if sorrow, too, had been her lot.

Not one experience of her life had I ever shared. Her mountaintops and valleys were as foreign to me as the surface of another continent, and whatever her troubles were seemed to me to be insignificant.

When the operator moved, my own face, too, was visible in the mirror; and suddenly I knew that my troubles were just as insignificant as hers if I could move away from them long enough to realize it.

Read Matthew 10:29-31.

Dear Lord,

I thank You that this lady whom I do not know and I are loved by You and are so well understood that even the hairs of our heads are numbered. I know that You have strengthened us both through the experiences of life and that though we are strangers to each other we are not strangers to You. I cannot comprehend the complexity of Your dealings with mankind, but I thank You for the inclusiveness of Your love. For Jesus' sake. Amen.

25. *Weeds*

My friend Ruthie is an excellent gardener. She also plants flowers in my soul. When I asked my prayer group to pray for God to guide my thoughts in writing this book and thinking of themes that all women understand, she spoke up.

"Grace, there is a little vine, a weed really, that I've been digging up all week. It is a fairly pretty little thing, but it reaches out its own little root system and multiplies so fast it chokes out all my expensive plants I've ordered to make my garden really beautiful. I've been thinking about that little vine all week."

As she talked I thought that little vine could be likened to sin in our lives. Then I remembered that Jesus had something to say about just such things in the explanation He gave of the parable of the sower. The seed that were sown among the thorns were choked out by the cares of the world and the deceitfulness of riches. By such things the word was made unfruitful.

Nothing could be truer of our lives. The pretty little blossoms of trivia that multiply take all our time and choke out the important things which God had meant to have grow and bloom. The bad thing about these little harm-

less, sometimes necessary, distractions lies not in their intrinsic wickedness or even uselessness, but in the fact that they masquerade as ultimate good and rob us of life's best.

I know a lot about these weeds. For years now piles of unironed clothes have taken precedence over calls to the lonely and ill and those who needed me. Cleaning house has taken precedence over kneeling in repentance and letting God cleanse my soul. Doing mundane duties has kept me from writing which I feel to be God's present task for me.

It takes some real gardening to keep the weeds of life cleared away so the lovely plants may grow. It takes the real Gardener to do this for our lives.

Read Mark 4:1-20.

Dear Lord,

We know You have planted the seeds of Your eternal love in the gardens of our hearts. Please uproot the weeds of the daily cares that choke out their fruitfulness that our lives may be beautiful and conform to Your plan and purpose for us. In Your name we pray. Amen.

26. *Penpoints*

The magic of a penpoint is incredible. With the point of a pen wars are incited. With the point of a pen peace is signed. With the point of a pen love is nourished. With the point of a pen it is destroyed. The same pen can sign a marriage license or a divorce decree.

We are much like pens ourselves. We are written with by whatever controls us. That to which we devote ourselves shapes the letters that form the words.

42

May the pen of our lives always remain in the hand of God to write upon the pages of our days the message of love so sorely needed by a world apparently devoted to malice and misery.

Read II Corinthians 3:1-6.

Dear Lord,

Take the pen of my life into Your hand and write upon the pages of my days Your words, not mine, I pray. Amen.

27. *Rhythm*

The heart beats and stops, beats and stops with a regular rhythm throughout our lives. We, too, must beat and stop, beat and stop if our efforts and inspirations are to flow with invigorating power into the bloodstream of our lives.

There is a time for speaking and a time for listening, a time for laughter and a time for tears, a time to love and a time to struggle with our hate, a time of sorrow and a time of joy.

In painting a picture it is the contrast of lights and darks that gives form and substance and shape to things. If we find it necessary to alternate color values to paint a picture, surely we can understand how God changes the color value of our life's experiences to shape and shade us into the people He would have us be.

Read Ecclesiastes 3:1-13.

Dear Lord,

Help us not to feel that we are failing You when the time to rest and renew our resources comes. Help us to feel Your rhythm of life and know that half its pulse is in the rest in the beat. Amen.

28. *Concordance*

I am not one of those chapter and verse Christians. About all the passage references I can be sure of are the Ten Commandments, John 3:16, the Beatitudes, and the Twenty-third Psalm.

Beyond this I have to look up references in the Concordance of my Bible, and my Bible has a limited Concordance. For nearly an hour now I have been trying to look up a very familiar verse of scripture and have not found it. I have even asked the Lord to help me remember where it is. Then like a sudden flash of light I got the point.

Many times each one of us is someone else's concordance in discovering the truth of God. Many times we are not faithful in all our listings, and when they look in us to find certain values that will help them to understand God in their own lives, they cannot find them. Instead of pointing them to a better way, we have no reference to what they really need; and they go away sorrowful, thinking the Christian faith does not contain their answer.

Read Matthew 7:21.

Dear Lord,

Help me to so know and follow Your commandments in my heart that those who are looking for You may see enough of Your spirit shining above my own imperfections that they may lay hold on eternal life. For Jesus' sake. Amen.

29. *What Moves You?*

Motivation is the catalyst of accomplishment. Without it life becomes a dull routine and no great things are even undertaken.

Deadlines are necessary if achievement is to be speedily made. Efficiency lies not nearly so much in repetition as in inspiration.

Motivation may be likened to hungers which must be assuaged—the hunger for love, for recognition, for security, for fame, for power, for wealth. These have led men to noble ventures and devastating debacles. They are powerful hungers, and all of them are hungers of the spirit.

In the last analysis it is the spirit of man that is his motivational lever. Set solidly upon the fulcrum of faith, there is no end to the loads the spirit of man can lift nor the good that he can accomplish, but for the fullest satisfaction even to the individual this fulcrum and lever must be used for larger than personal goals.

Selfish motivation is not enough. God's call to feed the hungry, visit the sick, help the widows and orphans, visit the prisoners, and spread the gospel to the ends of the earth must be heard and heeded if the needs of the world are going to be met in time to ward off nuclear annihilation.

Sometimes fear itself can be the catalyst. If this be so, then the world is in need of a healthy case of fear to make it exercise its faith.

Read Luke 12:29-31.

Dear Lord,

It is easy for me, a housewife, to understand the hungers of the spirit. I spend most of my time satisfying the bodily hungers of my family. I know how often children spoil their appetites for nourishing meals by eating candy before lunch. I know, too, that sometimes we try to satisfy the hungers of the spirit with the wrong things. Help me to instill in my children an appetite for the right kinds of

45

food for their bodies and their souls that they may in turn be able to feed the hungers of a starving world. Motivate us with Your love and fill us with Your power, I pray. For Jesus' sake. Amen.

30. *Storms*

Storms come up suddenly on lakes. They come up just as suddenly in our lives. A storm on a lake is a fearful thing if you are out in a rowboat. A storm in your life is doubly fearful if you are living under your own power.

It does not matter how ruffled with storm the lake may be, we are not fearful of safety as long as the motor is running and we are headed in to shore.

When the storms of life overtake us, fear does not prevail as long as the power of God throbs in our hearts and we feel His hand on the rudder of our lives.

> The skies though bleak and overcast
> Can never frighten me
> As long as throbbing motors bring
> Me safely home from sea.
>
> I will not fear the ocean's deep
> Nor tremble for my soul,
> Although I may not see the shore,
> If God is in control.

Read Luke 8:22-25.

Dear Lord,

When life's storms overtake us, help us to remember that You alone can still the waves. Amen.

31. *Love*

The human heart is born with an insatiable appetite for love.

In the steel and concrete machinery of our urbanization, all too often this appetite is fed on crumbs; and the malnutrition of the personality expresses itself in all sorts of deformed and crippled responses to life.

The Bible says, "God is love." A reawakened awareness of God is the first step toward nourishing this basic need of man.

Many of our disappointments in people stem from not recognizing their crippled responses to life as a lack of adequate nourishment of love in their hearts.

God does not expect the spiritually crippled, through genetic or environmental handicaps, to become saints any more than the crowd at a ball game expects amputees to make touchdowns.

Why, then, should Christians expect the impossible of those who cannot produce? Not until the crippled condition is corrected are any of us really able to run the race of life.

Read John 21:15-17.

Dear Lord,

Help us to look with love at the lives of others and to feed them with Your eternal love that their spirits may be well-nourished, strong, straight, and immune to the crippling spiritual diseases that result from malnutrition of the soul. In Jesus' name we pray. Amen.

32. *Life*

Jesus Christ in the normal everyday experiences of life comes to every person. We often fail to recognize His voice, or hearing, try so hard to understand that we lose sight of Him again in our intellectual calisthenics.

Oh, for the faith of a child who has not lost the capacity to take miracles at face value and see God in every little thing!

In spite of our usual miracle-blindness, there are a few magic moments each of us have when we are still aware. Women can hardly manage to look for the first time into the face of a newborn baby without being overwhelmed by the miracle of life.

To a New Baby

There you are—soft and warm and helpless,
An altogether lovely miracle of God,
Surrounded for awhile with His own wall of love,
Unable to maim or harm or fight,
Called only to learn and grow and get
Accustomed to all the strange new world
Before your tiny eyes.

Gradually you will pick and choose those
Things in life that will be yours.
May you not in the years to come
Cast off that wall of love around you now,
For truly it was meant to be
God's gift to you for life.

Read Luke 18:15-17.

Dear Lord,

When we stand awed in the presence of this tiny new
life and know that hidden here are talents and abilities
and concepts that will open as a rose if we carefully tend
and nurture the child, we pray for Your eternal adequacy
for this task. We know even as we pray that it will come
to us as miraculously as this new life itself if we just let
go and let Your love flow through us. For this assurance
we thank You. Amen.

33. *Limitations*

Man spends much of his time formulating and imposing
arbitrary limitations upon himself and others. Most of these
regulations are artificial and eventually succumb to nul-
lification with the passage of time.

God sets only a few limitations. Most of these are organic. Human genes can never be made to manufacture elephants, but man's ingenuity can create machines to do the work of herds of them.

God's limitations are actually capsuled potential, and this potential in every man must be released if we are to attain the stature to which mankind is called.

Be careful when you say "no" to a child's "May I." You may accidentally set your limitations, not God's, on his life.

Read John 14:12-14; Philippians 4:13.

Dear Lord,

We realize You have given all of us many more talents than we use, a great deal more love than we show, many more opportunities than we take advantage of. Please help us not to let fear and legalisms bind us and keep us from becoming what You mean for us to be. Amen.

34. *Predestined by Potential*

Our lives are more predestined than we believe. To begin with we are born *people,* not goldfish nor killer whales. We are mortal, limited in space and time to a tiny range of temperature. We have a specific size and weight which, though varying with age, limits to a great extent our ability to lift and grasp; this is the chief factor that governs our athletic prowess, or at least the sports in which we may excel.

Students of the behavioral sciences have developed complex batteries of tests to measure aptitudes in every field.

I wonder why it is that we in religion cling so desperately to the idea that we are the masters of our own fate and captains of our souls? We seem to be plagued with a superb egotism that blinds us to truth.

There is a call of God that runs so deep within us we sometimes never know it is there and think we do our bidding when we do His. It is this movement of God in all of life that is authority, and all our legalisms are valid only when they coincide with this authority of truth.

Some have sought to define this powerful pull of the spirit as predestination or have foolishly assumed that destiny's drive did not encumber them; "I make my own decisions," they often say.

Still the undeniable presence of a power beyond man is so obvious that the atheism of Marx cannot ignore it. Communists allude to it as the inevitable course of history. Earlier, more honest men were not afraid to acknowledge its source by calling it the providence of God.

We who invent our own watches sometimes forget *who* invented *time*. We who chart our own courses forget *whose* earth and sky the courses trace.

Let not the church diminish her power by forgetting *whose* she is.

Read Genesis 1; Matthew 25:14-30.

Dear Lord,

We thank You for the potentials of our lives and those of our children and all Your children everywhere. Help us as individuals to develop the potentials within us according to Your plan. Guide those who work with children and youth to help them discover who they are, why they are here, and where they are going. For Jesus' sake. Amen.

35. *Birthday Party Lists*

Birthday parties are a part of the heritage of happy memories mothers work hard to provide for their children. More important than the food or favors or games for a party is the list of friends to share the day.

Lists of names are very revealing. Have you ever noticed how many Marys and Marthas, Peters, Pauls, and Johns you count among your friends and place on party lists throughout your life?

It is easy to trace the origin of these names to those who heard and followed Christ long years ago, but did you ever see a child named "Rich Young Ruler"? Neither did I.

I have often wondered what his name was, that privileged young man who met Christ, longed to follow Him, asked the requirements, and lost his nerve because he thought the price was too high.

Two thousand years have passed. Compared to this day's riches the *rich* young ruler would seem poor indeed. For what to us would not seem wealth at all he gave up what perhaps could have been a place in history, a name, if you please, to ring down the ages the sort of man he was. We have an intimation that he could have been as great a man as Peter, John, or Paul; but his little hoard of temporal things blinded him to what Jesus really had to offer.

St. Paul's Cathedral in London pays homage to one who met the Master on the road to Damascus and followed Him. St. Peter's in Rome honors the fisherman who dared to leave his nets and follow Jesus. No one knows the plan the Master had for the rich young ruler. You and I can know the plan the Master has for us only in following Him.

Read Luke 18:18-25.

Dear Lord,

When we hear Your voice and know to heed it will mean giving up that which is of great value to us, help us to remember the rich young ruler and realize that *not* to follow demands the greatest sacrifice of all, for if we fail to follow we reject Your greater gifts. Amen.

36. *Home*

America is full of affluent homelessness. Few indeed are the children of this generation who know the stability of having watched a tree grow or having seen a hillside turn green in successive springs until the very leaves seemed to be their own and the dirt under their feet special stuff that was their private bit of earth.

Instead, today's children are constantly uprooted and moved to strange surroundings where trees grow imperceptibly in the short span of time that is theirs to watch; and they are lucky if one spring comes to the hillside in their sight. The earth is only dirt beneath their feet, and the walls of the house are not shadowed with the memories that make a house a home.

In a way the nomads had more actual homes than we. At least they took their tents with them and the rents and fades that blemished them were rents and fades of memories that were not obliterated by moving off.

Here we spend our lives in bits and snatches, and the enduring relationships of love and community and friendship become increasingly superficial. Sentiment wanes. Love loses its reality; and in a maze of ever-changing things the heart finds no rest.

We forget that most of the purchase price of a *home* must be paid in the coin of the heart. This is not counted in dollars and cents, but in loyalty, devotion, self-giving, and love. Without these, palaces are prisons. With these, caves can be castles.

America does not need better things nearly as much as she needs better people.

Read Proverbs 15:14-17; Micah 4:4.

Dear Lord,

The role of woman has always been to light the hearth fires of the home. Help me, a woman, never to forget the privilege and honor that goes with this task. Bless those who come into our house as well as those who live here. May we feed and warm and heal them; and when we move from one place to another, help us to carry with us the essence of our home. In Your blessed name I pray. Amen.

37. *The Significance of Self-Esteem*

There is nothing more basically essential to abundant life than a healthy self-esteem. This is not to be confused with the self-righteousness of the religious bigot nor the secular conceit of the worldly sophisticate. It is, rather, a deep inner assurance of one's own worth and adequacy which frees the individual to reach out in love and compassion and concern for others. True self-esteem is not the antonym of humility, but the confidence it takes to strive toward a worthy goal. Such confidence often results in that genuine humility that comes from rubbing shoulders with the great minds of the past and present.

Those who have never known the loss of self-esteem cannot properly appreciate its value. Neither can those who have never had it to lose. Only those who have experienced both confidence and lack of it during a lifetime can understand what a freeing thing is self-esteem and be sensitive to the hunger for it in others.

The orientals have a word for it in their concept of "saving face," but genuine self-esteem goes far beyond this. It has nothing to do with keeping up with the Joneses, although many choose this avenue in their attempts at achieving it. It has nothing to do with that extreme sense of competition that demands that one be always a winner in life. It is rather a state of spiritual well-being that unlocks the door to the prison of personal problems and lets an interest in others into the heart.

We live in an age when people are often uprooted and forced to leave behind all they have worked for and sought after, and to step into strange surroundings to start life all over again, often without the energy to try to make another place for themselves. The lost and lonely are all around us. One of the greatest services anyone can render is to lead someone from the darkness of a lost identity into the sunlight of acceptance and trust and hope. This is one of the few free gifts still left in life. It is a part of what Peter meant when he said, "Silver and gold have I none; but such as I have give I thee."

Read Philippians 4:13; John 6:1-14.

Dear Lord,

I am well aware of my shortcomings. There is so much I really want to do that I do poorly or not at all. Others about me seem far more talented and capable than I. Please help me to remember that our adequacy as people lies not in ourselves but in You. When I feel that I do not measure up, help me to be sure that You can take my little life and bless and multiply it, even as You did the boy's loaves and fishes long ago, and work wonders with it. Into Your hands I commit this day. Amen.

38. *Those Things We Tuck Away*

I was going through a box of stuff today. I call it "stuff" because it is such a conglomeration of things I had put away to help me remember.

There were travel folders from trips we had made, letters from friends, cards of sympathy and cards of congratulation, the little beads with our baby's name that had been worn on his wrist at the hospital, newspaper clippings, and lots of other memorabilia that wives are wont to stash away against the time when all they have left of life will be memories.

I was amused at some of the naive ideas I had jotted down some years ago, particularly those pertaining to my faith, but every now and then I came across a penetrating thought that I realized had stood the test of time.

The words that I had written no more fit my life now than the beads would fit the wrist of my teen-age son, except where they coincided with the eternal word of God. Somehow, though, the insights written there spelled the name of God as I had understood Him at that time, just as the beads of that bracelet still spelled my son's name.

I am sure it is always thus with words. The ones we write at one stage of life are not those we write at another. The faith that suffices in youth is not sufficient for age.

Just as a tree must extend its taproot deeper as it grows taller in order to weather storms, so the soul of man must ever delve deeper into the truth of God to grow straight and beautiful and bend with the wind without being destroyed.

Read Jeremiah 17:7-8.

Dear Lord,

I thank You for all the days of my life and the blessings You have sent every single day. As I look back I can see many winds of experience that have helped force my taproot of faith deeper into Your truth, and still I know that I have fallen far short of delving deep enough. There is so much to learn, Lord; help me to discover those truths that make life strong and good, able to bend with the wind without being uprooted. For Jesus' sake. Amen.

39. *TV*

There is abroad in our land today one of the most destructively subversive forces that we have ever faced. It does not stem from communism, but from a climate of cynicism and distrust that is being cultivated through every medium of communication that we use.

The newspapers have for so many years been headlining the criminal forces in our land that today's children are beginning to feel that this is the norm rather than the unusual in human behavior. This feeling is further imprinted on their minds by the constant exposure to every sort of crime on television. This may not be so bad when the issues of good and evil are clear-cut, but there is a growing tendency for anyone who looks as though he had washed his face in the last six weeks to be looked on with suspicion. In novels, movies, magazines, and more and more in general conversation, the moral indifference and spiritual numbness of our culture are so emphasized that it is a rare thing to encounter a character who is what he seems to be, especially if he happens to be a decent human being.

The truth of the matter is that a great many people are honorable and upright. The builders of any great culture are those who stand for something beyond their own selfish interest. Our country was made great by the hard work and sacrifice of many men and women who were not as concerned about their own safety as they were about building a nation that their children might enjoy. The freedom they sought was in more cases than not a freedom *to* worship, not a freedom *from* worship; a freedom *to* work, not a freedom *from* work; a freedom *to* vote, not a freedom *from* voting. We paint a false and misleading picture of our past when we let our youth think that their forebears were all rough and rowdy cutthroats and ne'er-do-wells. If a proportionate number of our pioneer men had spent as much time in saloon shenanigans as any Saturday night television fare would lead one to believe, this country of ours would still be an unpopulated wilderness.

In a day when so many seem to think the world owes them not only a living but a life of luxury without any responsibilities or restraints on their part, it is no wonder that our mental hospitals are full to overflowing. Man cannot live creatively in a cultural and ethical vacuum. So many influences vie for man's allegiance that he is all too often left at the end of the day with weary questions as to what he is, who he is, and what he is here for.

We need some good news coverage of the great things men do. It would be refreshing to have the statistics on the number of husbands who are faithful to their wives, and vice versa; to hear occasionally about the juveniles who not only are not delinquent but who are already making the world a better place for being in it.

If our way of life does not begin to show its good side to the public, the world which does not recognize our appetite for the sensational will judge us by the newspapers, movies, and TV reports of us. They will, in fact they have already begun to, accept us according to the vicious reports we publicize about ourselves.

Read II Timothy 2:15; Proverbs 26:20.

Dear Lord,

We pray for grace and power to live, to publicize, and to recommend the good life. We pray that You will touch the hearts of those who make the decisions as to what will be broadcast into the homes of our nation. Give to them the vision of what could be done for our nation with the tremendous communicative art at their disposal. Speak through our new technologies, we pray, that we may become strong and secure with understanding and wisdom that will stand the test of time. Amen.

40. *Repairs*

I can remember as a child thinking my parents could do anything. Mother still tells about the day I brought her the stem of a flower in one hand and the bloom in the other and said in utter confidence, "Mama, fix my buttercup." She also remembers the hot July day when I brought my favorite blanket to her and said, with beads of perspiration on my brow, "Mama, make my pink blanket cold."

There is a place in life for a simple childlike faith.

Amidst the complexities of earth, muddled by the partial human understanding of many things, a shouting and clanging and clashing of ideas, man needs a quiet place where the soul can be at home with God. He needs a sure and confident place of beauty where the little details of life fall away and the overwhelming orderliness of the universe rushes in to hush the trembling of the soul and let God stand revealed in all His power.

Sometimes this place is found on top of a mountain where the world falls away in the distance—trees become shrubs and ridges and finally shadows on the horizon, and a birdcall sounds louder than the traffic in the valley.

Sometimes this place is beside the still water which hides worlds of fish and sea things, with the water bending its surface to every breath of wind or break of pebble.

Sometimes this place is in the city where a blade of grass sticks up its sword in the crack of the pavement to remind us of the power in a seed.

Sometimes it is in the open, wondering eyes of a child, but always there is a place for meeting God if we would find Him, for in spite of His power and majesty, He truly is accessible to man, and God the Creator can repair life.

Read John 16:33.

Dear Lord,

Sometimes the confusion of the world with all its troubles overwhelms me. At such times help me to turn off a few of the motors around the house, even the TV, radio, and stereo, and take time to listen to Your voice, the birdcall that reminds me that You know even when a sparrow falls, the rhythmic beating of my own heart which keeps me alive though I never give it any thought. In these sure evidences of Your mercy let me take heart that I may know this is still Your world and it will never rest for long in the strident keeping of those voices bearing tales of woe. For Jesus' sake. Amen.

41. *Price Tags*

Ours is in many ways an impoverished nation seeking to satisfy with decaying material possessions the eternal longings of the soul.

The best things in life cannot be bought. The tingle of the cool air pin-pricked with stars on a winter's night, the crackle of a warm fire, the light in the eyes of those you love are all without price and of eternal value.

There are many commodities which cannot be assigned a dollar value. To try to reduce them to such terms is both futile and unnecessary. Who can put a price tag on a sunset or calculate in diamonds the brightness of a star? Who can say what a smile is worth or how far it travels? Who can adjudge in money the cost of courage, or sacrifice, or love?

There is a currency costlier than the coin of the country and of infinitely more value. It is minted with patience in the innermost recesses of the heart, and to be of value it must be spent with abandon in that marketplace of life which seeks not its own profit but that of others. It is a magic and ever-multiplying coin which only returns to the spender when it is given away.

It is sometimes called friendship, or charity, or compassion, or hope, or confidence, or courage. Its real name is none of these, but *love;* and love is of God, for God is love.

We have so many of our values mixed that we virtually trade diamonds for rhinestones almost every day. It takes alertness not to be misled by the price tags on certain things in life.

We must be wary lest we miss life's treasures in pursuing the commonplace.

Read Matthew 13:44-46.

Dear Lord,

Help us to know true values when we see them. We spend so much time reading price tags and accepting the evaluations that others place on life that we sometimes find ourselves knowing the price of everything and the value of nothing. Make us wise buyers in the marketplace of life, we pray. Amen.

42. *We Sell Sex Short*

I cannot believe that casual coitus is the way to satisfy the soul-stirring sex urge in the heart of man. Nothing in all creation is so beautiful, so basic, so evidently the creation of God as the love of a man for a woman.

On it all of life depends. Nothing is more miraculous, more healing, more enduring than the wholesome, healthy sex life of two people deeply in love. It is a shame that the adventure of promiscuousness has been so dramatized as to leave the impression that illicit sex is fun and that marriage has been so caricatured as to make it appear a dull duty.

People being what they are, it is no great achievement to woo an unstable person into a short-lived intimacy. It takes a great deal more glamour and finesse to make a long-term marriage into a romantic, glowing honeymoon; but the depth of affection and the freedom of total emotional expression of the latter over the former make it more than worth the effort.

It is great after sharing half a life together to stand with friends on a clear moonlit night, laugh gaily at their banter, feel your husband's arm around you, and hear your heart whisper:

> "They said it was a lover's moon
> That hung above the trees.
> The sky was black sequined with stars;
> There was a gentle breeze.
> I stood there bathed in silver light;
> And suddenly I knew
> It really was a lover's moon,
> For I stood there with you."

Read Ephesians 5:22-33.

Dear Lord,

Thank You for the Book of Ephesians with its excellent bit of advice to those who are married; it is a prescription that really works. I thank You, Lord, for the beauty and wonder of enduring love and for the children it has brought forth. Help me to be the sort of person who is worthy of love in this dimension. May I never forget that true love encompasses the soul as well as the body and that it is the most sacred and holy gift of life. May my love always bless my husband and strengthen him and make him whole. In Your blessed name. Amen.

43. *Gems of the Spirit*

Every now and then I straighten out my jewelry drawer. I use the term *jewelry* loosely because few of the items in the drawer would be classified as jewels by anyone but me.

Some of them are gems to me because they are reminders of the tenderness and love of the giver. I do not suppose any of them—except for one pair of earrings made of seeds that just seem to go with everything—were bought by me. But I am sort of a pin-and-earring person, and friends have bestowed upon me quite a cache of costume jewelry.

I find it difficult to throw any of it away because even if it does not go with anything and may be a little out of style, it reminds me of old places and old friends, of my children at different ages and of my husband's tender love. And then, too, some day I may just need that particular bauble to set off an outfit that I have yet to buy.

I have another jewel box. No one would recognize it as such. It is a battered notebook stuffed with bits of paper. It contains little lines of thought that have come to me at various times and places to add color and sparkle to the drabness of my day or to embellish with beauty a bright moment of joy.

Each line is the result of some particular need or concern or is a spontaneous spark of inspiration I recognized as coming from the heart of God. Most of them are not gems of wisdom, but they go with the designs of a great number of my days, and they may go equally well with some of yours.

★ The coin of the kingdom is minted in the human heart and pays dividends only upon being given away.

★ You cannot sing a song with just two or three notes— nor make a home that way.

★ You do not spell sex S-I-N, or vice versa.

★ You cannot adequately describe a rosebush after only inspecting a thorn.

★ Deadlines are catalysts of accomplishment.

★ The design in the needlepoint of friendship is worked one stitch at a time.

★ Sometimes our very difficulties shape us into the keys that will unlock the doors to abundant life for other people.

★ In our eagerness to eliminate the evilness of evil, we have accidentally obliterated the goodness of good.

★ The lens of love puts life in focus and enables us to see.

★ We become so enamored with the design of our days that when their pattern falls apart we fail to realize that in God's kaleidoscope of life the bits and pieces will form other patterns equally intricate and every bit as beautiful.

★ Dreading things is a lot worse than doing them.

★ You cannot cook a meal with food that is not there. No more can you feed your soul and fail to replenish your spiritual shelves.

★ The Lord does not like our leftovers.

★ Procrastination is the thief of time, and disorganization of life's daily details is its accomplice.

★ You cannot put God in a test tube; He won't fit.

★ Look with love at the lives of others.

★ Dare to be different.

★ God speaks in many ways; we often are just not listening.

★ My husband says some of my friends are all vogue on the outside and vague on the inside.

★ Plants must be watered daily; so must we.

★ Do not despair of the drive toward the good and beautiful in the heart of man as long as women flock to beauty parlors and sacrifice time and comfort to try to be more lovely than they are.

★ Only a few things really matter in this world. Among these few are faith and friends.

★ In your judgment of people they are noble or knaves, depending largely upon which factors of their makeup you choose to exaggerate or minimize. The kind of people you live with is entirely up to you.

★ In an age when money marks the measure of a man, it is not strange that we trust multimillionaires to manipulate the government.

★ Someone I meet today will be eager to hear the good news of Christ.

★ It does not matter what color a yardstick is as long as its thirty-six inches are marked off accurately.

★ The pinnacle of power can be a lonely place.

★ Every woman sees in children every child; and because she is a woman, her eyes light up and her heart reaches out. As long as a child can light a candle of love in the eyes of a woman, there is hope for the world.

★ The threads of our lives are intricately wowen into designs by the master Weaver, and it is only in looking back that we can recognize the pattern and see where the particular color and texture of our little strand of life fit in.

★ Every man's view of life is limited by the size and shape of the windows of his soul.

Read Proverbs 25:11-12.

Dear Lord,

I thank You for words in all their wonder. I thank You for the words that strengthen and those that admonish, for those that give hope and encouragement and open the doors of friendship, and for those that challenge us to tasks we tremble to tackle on our own. But most of all, I thank You for Your words which come to us from many sources: from the Bible, other books, sermons, the heart of friends, and from Your very presence as our hearts become attuned to hear Your words in prayer.

Lord, breathe into my words the wind of Your Spirit that I may not babble meaningless nothings along life's way. Help me at the times when You need me for Your spokesman to have Your word and fitly speak it, and thus add beauty to someone else's day. In Your blessed name, I pray. Amen.

44. *Fireside*

As I sit taking a breather after a busy morning, the green leaves of the geranium plant in the black iron kettle by our fireplace seem strangely out of tune with the wintery scene through the window beyond where bleak grey branches, brightened only by a few burnt sienna oak leaves, drip in the rain.

Yet here inside all is warm and colorful. African violets and poinsettias do not seem to even know it is cold outside. The crackling fire is cozy and the hearth secure.

I think the presence of Christ in the heart is much like this fire, warming and enabling the leaves of the spirit to flourish and shielding from the cold grey bleakness of the hopeless world all those who let Him in.

Read John 14:23; 16:24-33.

Dear Lord,

I thank You for the warm light of Your love that fills our home with joy and for the bright blossoms of children and their laughter that lightens our grey days. Help us never to forget that You are the source of all warmth and light and goodness and that our souls can only flourish in joy as the fire of love is kindled in our hearts by Your Spirit. For Jesus' sake. Amen.

45. *Stoplights*

Orientals and children cannot understand the slavery of American adults to the clock. We defend our schedules against all invasion and sometimes waste more time than we gain by being anxious over lost moments. Every one knows that lost moments are an inevitable aspect of today's complex culture.

It has been said that our forebears were not too disturbed if they missed one stagecoach—after all another one would be by in a few days, but we tend to have a nervous breakdown if we miss one section of a revolving door.

Wasting time waiting bothers me. Patience is not my virtue, nor ever has been. I have discovered a way to overcome this frustration by putting these minutes to good use. I have discovered God is only a prayer away, and these small snatches of time may be just the spiritual conditioners my soul needs.

I find that this theory is especially helpful at stoplights. More of my family and friends have been prayed for at the corner stoplight than ever would have been remembered if that light were always green. I have gotten to feel that it is God's little reminder to me to speak to Him more often. My life is richer for these little moments forced upon me in spite of my busy schedule.

When my husband heard me tell this to a friend, he said, "I hope you keep your eyes open; remember you're supposed to *watch* and *pray!*"—so I pass this bit of advice on to you for what it may be worth.

As is the nature of God, He took my little frustration and turned it into a joy.

Read I Thessalonians 5:16-28.

Dear Lord,

I thank You for the stoplight on the corner that used to be the very bane of my existence. I thank You for the many moments we have spent there together. I know they must add up to several hours now that I would not otherwise have spent aware of Your presence. If I took time here to thank You for each specific answered prayer, time would run out for me; but You know, Lord, that I am well aware of all those answers. Thank You, Lord. Amen.

46. *Decorating*

I spend a lot of time in decorating. Selecting colors and carpet and accessories to make our house a home takes weeks of hours, and I often wonder if this represents a squandering of time. Then I look outside my window and realize that God bothers with beauty.

In our utilitarian approach to life we fail to recognize the value of that which is intrinsically beautiful, and perhaps more useful because its beauty is there: The shine of bare wet branches in a rainstorm; the music of the rain as it falls on different surfaces making different sounds; the flight of a bird with its silent wings which put to shame the roar of jets and clamor of the motors man has engineered; the silent power of a peach seed in whose few grams of substance is hidden the ability to produce a tree and other seeds equally as magic; the beauty of the blossoms of those trees as they unfold in spring and the delicious beauty of their fruit in fall—all these are a tiny part of that holy beauty in all God's creation that is like unto God Himself. In each of these things there is a pattern, even in the days of our lives.

God guides our days, as surely as He guides the rest of His creation, by the plan hidden in us to produce His beauty, will, and purpose in our lives.

Read Psalm 27:4.

Dear Lord,

We thank You for life, for every day that dawns before us, shiny, new, and beautiful—whether its beauty be that of sunshine, snow, or rain. May we welcome every day and fill it to the full with Your love and Your will done. May each fleeting moment be made to count for a worthwhile purpose, that we may find that life abundant which You came to bring. Amen.

47. Middle-Aged Spread

I hate to think of myself as middle-aged, but I regret to say that if I am honest I must admit that I fall into this category. I hate to think of myself as putting on the pounds; but when my teen-age daughters invite me to do exercises with them or my boys say, "Mama, what do you weigh?" I realize that I am not as streamlined as I would like to be.

This is not, however, a consideration of bodily mis-proportions. What I want us to consider together is this: "Are our souls getting flabby?"

Are we carrying around extra pounds of prejudice and ounces of ill will? Are our doubts and fears and animosities toward others keeping us less than in spiritual trim? Do our faces show the tense lines of bitterness and fatigue instead of mirroring the gladness of our Master? If so, what exercises and diet program can we take to try to correct this condition?

First of all, we need plenty of water, that water of life which may be found in Jesus Christ.

Then we need the fruits of the Spirit, fruits are low in unwanted calories, high in vitamins and minerals and the natural energy-giving sweetness that makes us feel at our best. What are these fruits? Paul listed them for us in his Letter to the Galatians.

In order to eat of the fruits of the Spirit, we must exercise willpower in our thoughts, leaving out of our contemplation those things which make for envy, strife, and misery; thinking, instead, upon those things that are true, just, lovely, of good report, filled with virtue and praise, "For as [a man] thinketh in his heart, so is he."

If we walk with Christ in prayer and action, we will find our souls strengthened and rejuvenated; and though the outward woman perish, the inward woman will be renewed day by day.

Read Galatians 5:22-23.

Dear Lord,

Help me not to gorge myself on the rich desserts of self-indulgence which will burden me down in spirit, even as those added calories make me fat and slow me down;

71

but let me select the fruits of the Spirit for my soul's food that I may be trim and agile and ready to run well the race of life. For Jesus sake. Amen.

48. *Keys*

I never cease to be amazed at the keys God uses to unlock the doors of communication between His children.

There are many keys that are necessary in today's world. There are door keys and locker keys, trunk keys and car keys; and if other housewives are as scatterbrained as I am, more moments than they wish to admit are spent in searching for keys, sometimes in even trying to find the right key on a ring bearing a wide assortment of them, for everyone knows that only the *right* key will fit a lock and open a door.

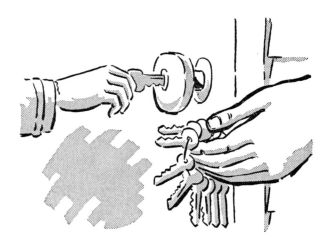

Most of the time we know where the keys are kept and reach for them almost automatically. Occasionally we stumble upon the right one. I think this is especially true in the area of communication.

There is a little thrill that goes with being handed the right key to a door you have never entered before. I have had this experience several times when being handed the key to a house that would for a few years be my home.

Sometimes God hands us keys in the normal routine of our days that unlock doors we had never planned to enter —the doors of friendship, understanding, and concern.

Today this happened to me. I had won a free, or almost free, trip to Florida and went to the store where my name had been drawn to see whether it was a bona fide deal. Upon meeting the manager and being assured that it was, I thanked him, introduced myself, and asked how long he had lived in our city. His was a new store in town.

He told me he was a newcomer, so naturally I asked him where he went to church. There was no church of his denomination in town; so he said he would take me up on the invitation to visit ours some Sunday soon.

This was not unusual; the unusual part was the conversation that followed during which I saw in this man a very deep and valid faith in God which meant a great deal to him as a source of strength and guidance in his life. I do not know whether he will come to our church or not, but I do know that God used that winning letter as a key to usher me into the presence of another Christian and that for that moment at least we shared our faith.

Life is full of such experiences; we just do not always take the time to recognize them. Often we hold the key in our hand and fail to even put it in the lock.

Read Matthew 16:19.

Dear Lord,

As I go about the busy routines of my days, make me aware of the keys You place in my hand and of the doors that can be unlocked by them. So often I run about doing this and that and never am aware of those about me who need to share their faith and thus find it strengthened. I often fail to recognize my own need in this respect. Thank You, Lord, for this day and its awareness. Amen.

49. Remodeling

When a house is remodeled, there must be a plan in the mind of the builder before the tearing down of the old and the building of the new can even begin. Just what to tear out and what to leave must be decided upon.

Our lives are like houses. As we grow older we find certain areas outmoded, unserviceable, inconvenient.

The rooms that harbor hate must be cleaned out, opened to the sunlight, warmed by love and made usable again.

No one wants to live in a dilapidated shambles, and our spirits cannot thrive if they dwell in the slums of the heart.

New materials are essential to replace the old. Boards eaten by the termites of hate, jealousy, and disillusionment must be replaced by the sturdy treated timbers of love, forgiveness, and hope.

With proper alterations, an old house can be a warm and wonderful place. An old soul may also become warm and comfortable, full of beauty and charm if the useless things are done away with and the good refurbished, polished, and shined.

Read I Corinthians 3:16.

Dear Lord,

Remodel my life, I pray, that I may be a fit temple for Your Holy Spirit. In the name of the Carpenter of Galilee. Amen.

50. *Supermarkets*

Life is in many ways like a supermarket. Its shelves are filled with a frustratingly wide assortment of things, and my basket is so small it will hold only a few. As a housewife I am forced to pick and choose the assortment of foods which will adequately nourish my family. These foods must be both within my monetary means and adapted to the tastes and needs of my family.

As a person I face a supermarket of ideas with which to fill my mind. Which ones I choose to feed upon will determine the direction of the development of my character and personality.

Some of the foods on the super-market shelves are fattening to the body, some cause allergic reactions, some are just not worth the money for the meager nourishment they afford. Some hold harmful things that nourish not at all.

It is just this way with life. Some of the cans on the supermarket shelves hold baby food and some hold food for mature adults. So it is with the foods of the spirit. Adults cannot thrive on baby food or vice versa.

In the supermarket some of the money must be saved for soap, toothpaste, and things like lipstick and shampoo.

In life's other areas we must also allow for that which cleanses and beautifies. For life is more than meat and the body is more than raiment.

Read I Corinthians 3:2; John 10:10; Philippians 4:8.

Dear Lord,

As I see the vast array of ideas on the market shelves of life, let me not be misled by the brightness of the packages and thereby spend all life's currency of time on the harmful or even the unessentials of life and fail to pick up the qualities of spirit that nurture the soul. May I instead select the fruits of the spirit that the hungry souls at our house may be fed with delicious helpings of all that is good in life. For Jesus' sake. Amen.

51. *Reminders*

Yesterday I dashed into a local store to look for an Easter blouse for our little girl. I had only a minute or two to spend; so I did not bother to wait for the elevator on the way down from the children's department.

When I started down the service stairs, my foot slipped. I stumbled halfway down the flight, finally catching myself on the rail with one hand and my chin.

For a few minutes I did not realize my chin was cut and bleeding. I was too thankful that no bones were broken to check the bruise. Even when I found the cut, I did not panic because of my relief at not being a stretcher case.

In the rest room a nurse from the emergency room at the hospital happened to be chatting with a friend. She assured me no stitches were required and applied a band-aid. I went on my way, thankful for my healthy skeletal structure and for that handy ministering-angel nurse.

Not until later did it dawn upon me that I had been down that flight of steps dozens of times over a period of years with no mishap, and never once had I stopped to be thankful. I wonder why we have to have troubles to make us remember God's blessings.

Read Psalm 116:8-9.

Dear Lord,

For the blessings of safety I take for granted every day, I thank You. Help us to be as aware of Your blessings and grateful when things go right as we are of our need of You when things go wrong. Amen.

52. *Cleaning Out Our Attics*

My attic is entirely too full for someone who moves as often as I do. There are boxes that have not been opened since we arrived at the place we lived three moves ago. Quite obviously I can well do without the contents of those boxes.

Why is it then that I find this stuff so difficult to dispose of? I can neither bring myself to sell it, give it away, nor throw it away.

When I see the clutter, I can tell how ridiculous this is; but when I open the boxes, I find each item was dear to some period of my life. It was significant and cherished and I hate to part with it.

Sometimes I think my mind and heart are equally encumbered. Outmoded ideas are stuffed away there. Many of the memories we cling to are only clutter. Many are ruined by the moth and rust of time. Many were not worth treasuring in the first place. Old frustrations, fears, and bitterness should have been thrown out immediately.

We spend our time accumulating life's experiences in the same way we spend our money accumulating things. And every housewife knows that among her treasures are valuable gifts bestowed upon her by others. This is true of life's experiences also.

The experiences we hold most dear are often those given us by God through loved ones. Such cherished gifts we neither can nor should get rid of. Their value grows when the value of many other things diminishes.

When we clean out the attic of our soul, we must be careful what we keep and what we throw away.

Read Hebrews 12:1.

Dear Lord,

Help me to separate the good from the worthless that my life may not be weighted down by unessentials. Amen.

53. *Telephones*

In a world blessed with the greatest communications system in history, technologically speaking, it seems impossible that one of our major sociological problems is lack of communication.

What is wrong with us?

Telephones and other communicative instruments are just that—instruments, not messages. Before they can be of value, there must be a message sender, a message receiver, and a message to be transmitted from one to the other.

When we use the telephone, it is essential that we know where the person we want to talk to is and the correct number for that phone. In our interpersonal relationships the same is true.

It is impossible to really communicate with someone if we have no idea where he is in his thinking, his emotional development, and his outlook on life. We have to dial his number before the channel of communication will be open. It is impossible to really communicate until we have an answer at the other end of the line. It is essential in any conversation to be a good listener.

It is impossible to really communicate unless we have something to say. Like television and radio, the messages we would share in personal conversation or over the phone can easily be cut off by those who are bored with the production. The music one generation prefers is not what appeals to another. So it is with the tunes of our lives. Overtures of friendship may be made to the wrong rhythms and be cut off by one who really needs a friend.

Communication is much more than a broadcast. It is a dialogue. Even in situations where verbal dialogues are impossible, spiritual dialogue is necessary. No speaker of real merit is unaware of that electric current of rapport that he senses from the expressions on the faces of those he speaks to. If the lively look leaves, the speaker had better change tempo and couch his thoughts in words that get across.

God has something to say to man today. He says it mostly through other people. This necessitates the involvement of the human instrument both to send and receive His messages. Much of the misunderstanding of the will of God can be traced to poor connections, static, and other human interference that make the sound of the voice of God unintelligible.

As God's instruments we can keep in shape through prayer, study, and most of all the exercise of love so that we will be adequate channels of His grace.

The next time you pick up the phone, listen to see if God is speaking through you; then listen to the one you are talking to and see if you hear God speaking through him. If not, when you hang up the phone, go to your closet and pray. Maybe there is interference in you, God's instrument.

Read Psalm 19.

Dear Lord,

I thank You for the gift of the telephone which enables us to talk to those we love both near and far away. My life is often enriched by the messages that come to me over this little instrument I hold in my hand. Let me be an instrument in Your hand that the words of comfort and hope and encouragement that come from You may be heard by those I love and those You love. Amen.

54. *Contact Lenses*

I have wanted contact lenses ever since they appeared on the market. For many years, however, I only needed glasses for long periods of reading, sewing, or meticulous work. Since I only used reading glasses and was forever putting them down and forgetting where I had put them, my husband said firmly, "No, I'll not buy contacts. The way you lose glasses you wouldn't be able to keep up with contacts for a week." There was so much truth to this that I did not insist.

Then my eyes got worse. I had to have not only reading glasses, but some to help me just plain see. I was seeing mustaches on the members of the choir—the lady members!

It took bifocals to do it. Once I became adjusted to the break in the vision sections I could see better because I wore them all the time, but I just hated wearing them because I do not like glasses.

Finally, my sweet husband said, "I have a friend who'd like to try making you some bifocal contacts."

I was delighted. The examination was easy. The lenses that I tried in the office were not too painful, and I looked forward to my lenses coming.

When they came, I went to the doctor's office. With the help of the doctor and his secretary, I was able to get them in and tolerate them for awhile. After several practice sessions I was allowed to bring them home.

Then I stuck them in the drawer, lacking the nerve to put them in alone. Yesterday I finally had the nerve to try them. I tried again and again but could not place them right. I blinked them out, put on my old glasses, and was a little disgusted at my lack of determination and my inability to get them in alone.

Not giving up, however, I tried again today. After many efforts I finally got them in correctly and can see. They are only a mild discomfort, and I believe that in time I will become accustomed to them. When I do, I will be able to see much better than with my normal eyes.

Religious faith is a lot like contacts. It is not something easily seen, but it provides clearer sight provided each part is in the proper place.

I think all too often people pop a bit of religion into their lives. It gets under life's lid or in a corner and is only an irritant, not a clarifier of life.

Religion must be in the heart through which all of life is seen before it can help anyone bring his experiences into their proper focus. To see life and its problems through the eyes of Christ, His lens of love must come between us and what we see so that we can properly interpret the scenes of life.

Many people who call themselves Christians have a Christianity that they wear all the time but which makes them feel so unattractive that they lose their winsome appeal, or they have a religion that is lost just at the time clear vision is essential. The lenses we put into our lives in the way of responsibilities assumed in the name of Christ may not show to others, but they should help us understand more clearly the meaning of His message for us. At first those things He calls us to do for Him may be irritating and uncomfortable, but soon we become accustomed to the inconveniences, and the view of life we have through His will working within us is so clear and beautiful that we forget the discomfort His truths give us.

Only those who get Christ into their hearts, discomforting as it may be, can correct some kinds of handicapped vision.

There are several similarities between any glasses and spiritual vision. Both have to be used, looked through, to make any difference. Both are sometimes uncomfortable. Both enrich life in the long run.

Read Luke 11:34.

Dear Lord,

Help me to see the needs of the world clearly with Your eyes that I may be able to truly say, "Where I was blind, I now see." And after I have seen, Lord, help me to meet those needs to the best of my ability, empowered by Your love. For Jesus' sake. Amen.

82

55. *Mirrors*

I spend a lot of time cleaning mirrors. The surface blemishes soon wipe off, but most mirrors have slight imperfections that no amount of cleaning will correct. These blemishes always distort reflections.

Our lives are much like mirrors, giving back distorted images of God. I wish someone could say to a God-hungry world, "Do not let your concept of the heavenly Father depend upon the reflection you see of Him in Christians' lives. The church is often like a Hall of Mirrors at a fair, giving many a distorted picture of God to a hungry, seeking world."

Then I see myself, rag in hand, standing there polishing; and I wonder what a God-hungry world would see in me.

If I could see the reflection of the kind of person I would most like to be, it would be a serene and loving person through whom God's healing power could flow to make life bright and beautiful for those around me. I really *want* to reflect God's love. This is my goal; but alas, I fear that I am actually too often a contentious grouch, determined to have my own way, and not even taking time to find out what others need of me.

Read I Corinthians 13:12; James 1:22-25.

Dear Lord,

Since I seem unable to smooth out the rough places in my personality by myself, I give myself to Your forgiving love and pray that You will use me as a mirror of Your grace in spite of my many blemishes. In Your own blessed name I ask it. Amen.

56. *Beauty*

Who can define beauty? Is it an especially attractive combination of features that compose a lovely face or a figure proportioned to a classic grace?

Is perfection of form beauty's prerequisite, or is beauty essentially a matter of the soul?

I have seen beauty in the wrinkled eyes of the elderly, in the tender touch of an elderly husband's hand on an equally elderly wife's arm. I have seen beauty in the gladness of a baby's smile and the tender tear of a mother.

Beauty is that intangible aura of interest and enthusiasm that makes some lives vibrate with an irresistible magnetism that has little to do with the shape and size of facial features, physical proportions, or intellectual prowess.

It shines in the faces of little babies, eager youth, and crinkly age. It is a touch of God in the life of man and arouses in the heart of all who are not blind a response that is essentially a response to life itself.

Some say that beauty is in the eye of the beholder. This may be true, for beauty, like laughter, sorrow, or joy, knows no language barrier.

It is a nebulous halo that graces many combinations of facial features and makes them shine. It seems to be reflected from the brilliant light of love within the heart. It is at best a holy thing, a portion of God's love spilling out into life.

As I sit beneath the hair dryer, I realize that no matter how the fashions change, not one of us who swelters here in silence will be one bit lovelier than the light we capture and radiate from our souls.

In trying to express this glowing aura, Renaissance artists of many lands painted a golden circle around the heads of saints and the patrons of the arts that they might go down in history as among the beautiful and good. We do not have our portraits painted in the guise of saints any more, but every woman here is working hard on her visible halo. I wonder what the world would be like if we all spent this much time shining up the halos of our hearts.

Read Matthew 5:14-16.

Dear Lord,

You know that every woman desires to be beautiful, yet I have never known one who was really satisfied with her outer appearance. I fear, Lord, that You are a lot more concerned about our inner beauty. Please take away the ugliness within us.

Wash away the grime of life that dulls the brightness of our souls. Fashion us into the people You meant us to be so that no matter what assortment of physical features look back at us from our mirrors on the wall, Your love will be reflected in the mirrors of our lives. For Jesus' sake. Amen.

57. *Moving*

There is a great difference between a group of houses built in close proximity and a neighborhood.

I stood at the window of the house that had been our home for nearly two years and looked out at the same group of houses I saw there when we moved in. The well-clipped lawns and flowering trees bespoke the efficiency and good taste of the people who lived there.

The scene was the same, only this time I did not look at a collection of architectural triumphs, but at a neighborhood. The people had names and faces, and there were the bonds of shared experiences that bound us together.

They were neighbors, and their friendship sheltered our hearts as surely as our house roof sheltered our home.

We were on the brink of another move, and I did not want to leave these neighbors. The house that had seemed so cold and unhomelike had held enough laughter and tears, warmth and love in the intervening space of time to make it home.

The walls were not as fresh as they were when we moved in. Here and there was a scuff where eager running feet had kicked too high. The rugs showed the marks of many feet that had passed over them in the pursuit of life. It had acquired a homey, lived-in look that made the lovely furniture inviting and the items of decor reminders of the fun we had had in living there. The phones had finger marks from conversations that had brought us heart to heart with people we had learned to love.

Of all the difficult hurdles of our present age, I think the multiple uprootings of families is the worst. It remains to be seen whether the children we shift from place to place will become adults more eager to make friends and more aware of human values, or whether they will build barriers against the onslaughts of love and friendship in order not to be further hurt when leaving time comes. Maybe they will be, like the nomadic Israelites, more aware of the plight of the stranger and more hospitable in welcoming him.

No doubt it will depend largely upon the child and upon the parents who have the choice of rearing him in a succession of houses or in a succession of homes, among strangers living close together or in many neighborhoods of friends.

Read John 14; Psalm 146:9; Exodus 23:9; Matthew 25:35; Ephesians 2:19; Hebrews 13:2.

I suggest more references than usual because it will be well to be reminded that God has much to say to us wanderers on this subject.

Dear Lord,

You know how I long for roots and my own home. I want familiar walls for my children to remember and the presence of friends whose lives I have shared long enough to really love. Lord, I feel a need in my heart to sit under my own shade tree and have a little land that belongs to me. Help me to be committed enough to You and my husband and his work not to mind moving so much. In this very act of moving You have blessed our lives with far more friends than we would have ever known otherwise. Let me remember this when we say our last good-byes here. Please give us traveling grace and open hearts to face the future. Amen.

About the Author

Grace Russell is the wife of the Reverend Henry E. Russell, pastor of Broadway United Methodist Church in Paducah, Kentucky. A native of Tennessee, Mrs. Russell attended Lambuth College, Jackson, Tennessee, and is a graduate of Southern Methodist University. She is an art major, and presently teaches art privately.

The Russells have five children: a daughter who is married and teaches school, a daughter and a son who are college students, a son in high school, and a daughter in the seventh grade. The Russells have served churches in Texas, Tennessee, Kentucky, and in England, where Mr. Russell preached in the Albert Hall of Manchester as a summer exchange minister.

Besides taking care of a parsonage family of seven, Mrs. Russell has served in many capacities in civic and church organizations.

A new realization that God, love, and friends are the real values of life inspired Mrs. Russell to write *Rings and Things.*